I0487969

How I Made $50,000

A Year, Part-Time,

Cleaning Gutters.

A Low Cost, High Profit
Money Making Business

By W.H.Griffin

Legal:

No part of this publication may be reproduced or transmitted in any form, or by any means, electronic, mechanical, photocopying, scanning, or otherwise.

This publication is to be used as an informational source only. It is intended to provide real life experience of the author. It is not intended as a business plan nor should it be viewed as such. While the author has made his best effort in preparing this book, he makes no representations or warranties with respect to the accuracy or completeness of the contents of this book. Laws and practices vary from state to state and if legal or other expert advice is required, the services of a professional should be sought. The author and publisher specifically disclaim any and all liability that is incurred in the use or application of this book.

Dedication:

This book is dedicated to anyone who has the motivation to improve their situation in life, whether it's financial or otherwise. It always starts with the first step.

Acknowledgments

To every person who has offered me advice, encouragement, life or business experience or friendship. I thank You.

Contents

Introduction

Introduction

Congratulations on taking that first step in joining the ranks of the small businessman. Although this isn't a very glamorous job, it is a highly profitable one. When I would tell people that I cleaned gutters, you can imagine some the responses I would get. Some would laugh at me, some would seem half-heartedly interested, others would move away from me as quickly as possible. That's ok, because I was laughing too, all the way to the bank!

Years ago I worked for a company as a house painter. It was a really grueling job for the money. I spent five days a week scraping, priming, painting, often in the blazing sun. And at the end of the week I would have little to show for all my hard work.

On occasion, while we were on a job, a homeowner would ask if we would clean the gutters while we had the ladders up against the house. The boss would always oblige, for a fee, of course! Now it didn't matter to me whether I was scraping, painting or gutter cleaning as I was getting paid by the hour. As we were packing up after completing a painting job in which we also had cleaned the gutters, the homeowner had to leave to run some errands. She couldn't find the boss so she asked me to give him a copy of the bill and a check for the balance due. Now on that bill was a charge for painting and a charge for gutter cleaning. So not only did I get to see how little I was making for the painting , but how much the company was making for gutter cleaning. The charge for cleaning the gutters was $125.00, and it only took me an hour.

I think my brain may have actually grown new synapses right at that very moment.

$125.00 for an hours work. It was like a Mantra that kept repeating in my head over and over. If I could clean three homes in one day, I could make more than painting all week ! And if I could keep busy three to four days a week I would make more in one week, than in one month .But ,would there be enough work? That was the important question.

As I investigated further I found that people would actually prefer to paint a house, rather than clean the gutters. It's usually a messy job, working at heights on a ladder. But that's why there is such a demand for professional gutter cleaners. Let's also look at demographics. In the United States there is a large ageing population. That ageing population gets larger every year. As people get older they tend to not want to go up any ladders if they don't have to. So what homeowner or businessman wants to go clean their gutters? The answer is, not many.

Gutter cleaning is also maintenance that needs to be done on either a yearly or bi-yearly basis. This is good for establishing a solid customer base. <u>Repeat business!</u> Not having to constantly find New customers is Key in this business.

As you will be able to tell from reading this book, this isn't some slick marketing hype, or a book full of useless business graphs and models used solely as filler pages.

This is a book about how I found a way to make great money, part-time. Hopefully you can use some of this information to start your own business. So read on fellow entrepreneur.

Chapter 1

Chapter 1

Setting up the Business

1.Naming the business

One very important aspect of any business is the company name. When choosing a name try to make it something people will remember, try to keep it short, and make sure it doesn't mislead people. Also make sure no one else is using the same name.

When I first started out I placed an ad in the local paper that looked like this:

Gutters cleaned

Call   anytime

xxx-xxx-xxx

I didn't get one phone call from this ad. My next ad looked like this:

Griffin Gutters

Gutters cleaned and repaired

All debris removed from site

Insured

xxx-xxx-xxx

So which ad would you call? If you look like a solid business entity you will get more work.

2.Hiring the Professionals

Laws vary from state to state so it will be up to you to find out what's required by law in your area.

The first professional I went to see was an accountant. He helped me do a lot of things that I had no idea needed to be done. We set up business bank accounts, decided what type of business I would be running. A sole-proprietorship is the most common, but there is also an LLC or getting incorporated, etc. He made sure the right papers got filed to the right people. He also showed me how to set up my accounting, which means keeping track of money coming into the business and what's going out. The more organized you are when you go see the accountant at tax time, the less money it will cost you. For him, time is money, your money!

My next stop was to go see about insurance. I simply called my automobile insurance agency, they also have a commercial business division. They explained to me what policies I would or should need. Any type of business needs a liability policy .Lets say your on a jobsite and the wind blows your ladder over and it lands on a clients nice Mercedes In the driveway. Right about now you'll be glad to have that insurance. The most damage I ever did was to put my ladder through a few windows. An out of pocket expense, but still, I slept better at night knowing I would be covered if anything catastrophic happened. Having medical insurance is also a necessity when your working on ladders all day. Talk your insurance agent, they will explain it all. The good thing about having insurance is, it will get you a lot more business. Most businesses that hire you will require you have insurance. This is going to separate you from the kid down the block. No one wants to chance having the liability of an uninsured contractor working on their property.

Another key player in any business is a lawyer. Go see a lawyer and have a chat. Maybe there's something your accountant or insurance agent didn't address that he will pick up on. You may want to have contracts written up specific to the type of business your in. You may want to keep him on retainer in case any litigation arises. Usually the first consultation is free, so like I said, go have a chat.

So right about now you're saying; "Wait! I just want to go clean gutters and make money; I don't want to get involved with all these professionals." Think small and be small, go about it the right way and you will make more money!

Chapter 2

Chapter 2

Equipment Needed

Basic equipment list:

1. A vehicle

The first thing needed is a vehicle to transport yourself and all the equipment to and from the jobsite. A pick-up truck is ideal for this, although I have seen many gutter cleaning companies that use a van, and I have even seen a few old station wagons being used. But hey, If its road worthy and safe, it will do.

2. Ladders

An assortment of ladders will be needed. I started out with only three ladders, a 36', 16' and a step ladder. I usually only cleaned one and two story houses, so I didn't need anything higher.

Now let me make an important point here. Buying good quality ladders and making sure that they will support you safely is very important. Knowing how to handle ladders is an important issue also. You must know the proper way to put a ladder up on a house, and take it down safely. Read the following story it will explain why ladder safety is so important.

I talked to a client on the phone and booked a gutter cleaning job for the next morning. I showed up as planned and put up my ladder against the back of the home. The driveway sloped down from the front of the home down to the back. It was a little higher than I liked to work, but my ladder was more than sufficient to handle it. As I started to climb up the ladder, I heard some sobbing from behind me. The homeowner was there, in a wheelchair, his wife beside him and they were hugging each other. I inquired if everything was ok. They explained to me that the gutter I was about to work on had not been cleaned in three years. Three years ago the husband had tried to clean them, but on this section of the house, the ladder wasn't quite high enough. You can probably guess the outcome. He over extended himself by climbing too high on a ladder that was too short. He fell off the ladder and is now paralyzed. It's a sad story but the lesson is, have the right piece of equipment for the job and know how to use it.

3. Ladder racks

These are used to support the ladders on the vehicle. It keeps the ladders from damaging your vehicle and gives you someplace to tie the ladders to during transport.

4.Ladder stabilizers

Ladder stabilizers bolt to the top of a ladder and is an accessory with wide tubular arms and non-skid rubber pads that grips a house wall, increasing both a ladder's stability and your "reach" working aloft. Using stabilizers will give you a very safe working angle to gutter. I recommend these be put on all ladders.

5. Hoses and Hose nozzle

I always carried two 50 foot hoses and a nice hose nozzle that was capable of producing a strong jet spray. Most of the time I was able to use the homeowners hoses, but sometimes the hoses wouldn't be hooked up yet. Always better to come prepared, just make sure the water is turned on in case the homeowner isn't going to be home.

6. Debris bucket and s hook

I used a 5 gallon bucket to put all the gutter debris in, and an s hook to hang the bucket off the ladder. If you toss the gutter debris all over the lawn and bushes, chances are you wont be getting called back. Be Neat!

7. Trash barrels

I always carried two barrels to take away all gutter debris.

8. Gutter debris rake

This is used to extend your reach and either push or pull gutter debris to one spot. Doing this means the ladder won't have to be re-positioned as much. Although this item is available in home supply stores I made my own out of a broom handle and a block of wood screwed to one end, simple and efficient.

9. Plumbers snake

I used this to unclog the elbows at the end of the gutter. If this doesn't work; the elbows will have to be taken apart and cleaned.

These are all the basic tools I used to get started. The largest

investment was a vehicle and ladders. As I started to make money I

purchased more tools as needed.

Chapter 3

Chapter 3

What are gutters?

Gutters protect a home against it worst enemy, water. A gutter system is used to take water from the roof and divert it away from the foundation. A properly installed and maintained gutter system will help prevent water from getting into basement, frost heaves on driveways and walkways, staining of siding, soil erosion, and fascia and rafter ends from rotting out.

There are basically three types of installations being done today. Seamless aluminum, which is the most common. These gutters are manufactured on the job site. Wood gutters, not as common today and very expensive. Plastic, common at most home improvement stores. You will also see copper gutter systems. These are very, very expensive. Not many people are installing them today, but I came across quite a few old installations.

The maintenance on aluminum gutters is fairly easy compared to wood gutters. With aluminum gutters its clean them, check for leaks or repairs, make sure water is diverting properly. Wood gutters on the other hand will have to be cleaned, let them dry, and come back and oil them to prevent the inside from splintering.   I used linseed oil on the wood gutters and it worked well. Plastic gutters are inexpensive to install, but have a lot more seams as they are usually sold in 10 ft lengths. More seams mean more possible leaks. The plastic also becomes brittle over time. Whenever I came across old plastic gutters in really bad shape I would suggest to the customer that they upgrade to seamless.

Chapter 4

Chapter 4

Getting business

Newspapers are a great way to advertise. Some larger newspapers own a whole bunch small newspapers, and they will give you a package price to advertise in all or just some. This always worked well for me. Call your local newspaper and inquire about rates for the areas you want to work in.

Coupon mailers always worked for me. You've seen this right? It's usually a large envelope stuffed with business advertising or coupons. I used these and offered a 10%discount with coupon. People love a deal and I could always count on getting business this way. The coupon mailer company also designed my coupon for me.

Contact real estate offices in your area. Send them a letter explaining who you are and what you do. Include 4 or 5 business cards with your letter. A real estate agent will try and get any edge they can to sell a house .If an agent shows a house to a potential buyer and there are weeds growing out of the gutters, it's usually a red flag indicating the previous homeowner did not maintain the property properly. Nine times out of ten the agent would ask me if I did any other work like painting or repairing things. Let me tell you ,once you help sell a house for a real estate agent, your name is guaranteed to be passed around and networked.

Townhouse and condo complexes   are another great place to get work. Homeowners pay a fee each month so that they won't have to take care of any maintenance on the property. The fee usually covers snow plowing, trash removal, lawn maintenance, and yes, gutter cleaning. Contact the rental or sales office and inquire about putting a bid in for cleaning the gutters. As I mentioned earlier, they WILL ask you for an insurance binder. Some of the complexes I worked at used a Management company to handle all the maintenance. Some of these companies managed multiple complexes, and they may ask for a bid on those as well. The great thing about working at these complexes is, there's a lot of gutter to clean and all the work is in one location. I usually had 4 to 5 complexes to clean on a yearly basis and I loved it. Money in the bank as they say.

The local printed phone book is another advertising medium. Although, because of the internet, it's not as popular today as it once was. People still use it, especially for the business advertising section, or yellow pages as it's referred to. Some people are just not computer savvy or don't own a computer, so they will go to the phone book. I advertised in three different phone books. I picked out the most affluent city and towns around my area and targeted these areas.

The Internet seems to be the most popular way people search for information. You may want to start your own website. Just like your company name, you should think long and hard about a website name. It would be great if your company name and website name were the same. You could use your website name in all your advertising. Its great to know how many people actually visit your website so make sure you ad some sort of traffic counter on site. You can collect all your clients e-mail addresses and remind them to schedule a cleaning via an e-mail. Submit your website to the top search engines, which is usually free. If you're computer literate you can probably handle all that is involved in getting online, but it wouldn't hurt to seek out someone or some company that will build your website and possibly maintain it for you.

Chapter 5

Chapter 5

Typical jobs and pricing

In my many years of gutter cleaning, I have come across every known situation to man that there is. From the homeowner who called me twice a year for cleaning, and there was never anything in the gutter. I mean, it was spotless every time I showed up. I told the homeowner that twice yearly wasn't necessary, or even yearly wasn't necessary. There were no trees within a 100 yards. But the homeowner wanted piece of mind, so I showed up twice yearly to give the gutters a quick spray with the hose.

Then there are homeowners on the opposite side of the spectrum. They check their calendars and decide its been twenty years since the last gutter cleaning, so they must be due for a cleaning. You Will want to charge more for this type of cleaning as it will take a lot longer.

The most common jobs I went to were single story capes and two story colonials. Sometimes they had additions on them, sometimes not. The criteria I used to determine what price to charge was as follows:

What type of home is it?

How many additions?

When was it cleaned last?

What type of gutter is it?

Level lot or does it drop off at all?

So lets assume I get a call from a prospective client, they tell me they have a one story cape or maybe it's a two story colonial with aluminum gutters, the last cleaning was a year ago, they have one addition and it's on a level lot. This a typical maintenance call.

Being able to give a price range to a client over the phone saved me a lot of time and money. My typical price range was $50 -$100 for a cape, and $75-$175 for two story colonials. I charged a higher price if they hadn't been cleaned for some time, then I would offer a lower price if they used me on a yearly basis. I was Always thinking of repeat business!

I also called other gutter cleaning companies in the area to ask about their rates to make sure my rates were not too high or too low.

Pricing large jobs like condo or townhouse complexes, you may want to give a little bit of a discount on the price since your doing volume work at the same location. They're still money makers even while giving a discounted price.

On almost all cleaning jobs I wore a tool belt so that I could carry with me one of the most vital pieces of equipment I needed, BEE SPRAY! Yes, on some jobs, you will encounter an angry hoard of bees or wasps, better to be prepared. Some of the other things you will encounter are bird's nests, squirrels, and I have even found frogs up in the gutter. I have no idea how they get up there, but you will also find an assortment of baseballs ,boomerangs ,hockey pucks and other things that will have you shaking your head and saying, "how the heck did this get up here"?

One of most dangerous hazards I would run across on almost every job was electricity. The electrical line that runs from the street to the house usually connected to the house on the corner where the gutter and downspout are. Let's think about this for a minute, I would be working on an aluminum ladder that's grounded to the earth, the gutter is made of aluminum and sometimes had water in it. So the gutter, water and ladder are all conductors of electricity. Moving slow and careful in this area is very important!

Chapter 6

Chapter 6

Make More Money

with Repairs.

I have found that on many cleaning jobs I would run into some type of repair that would be needed. If you are able to show up when scheduled, clean the gutters and do it neatly, and do any repairs as needed, then you will get a lot more work. One of the homeowner's most common complaints was that a contractor would never show up as scheduled, or couldn't finish the job, requiring another contractor to come finish it. Being able to do small, fast, easy repairs will help your bottom line and make you look very good in the homeowner's eyes. This translated into more money for me, and more referrals.

The most common repair I ran across was replacing downspout elbows where it connected to the gutter. This is especially common with metal or galvanized elbows. These are usually used with wood gutters. The elbows would get jammed with debris and after a while of sitting, will rot out. I carried all different kinds and styles of elbows as well as downspout.

Here are some examples of other repairs :

Adding extensions on bottom of downspout to get the water away
   from foundation.

Replacing downspout that was damaged or rotted

Replace strap hanger or wire hanger on downspout

Replace gooseneck

Seal leaks on corners or end caps

Re-attach gutter pulling away from house, add hangers as needed

Add drip edge to roof line so all water goes in gutter and not behind it

I usually charged $20 to $30 dollars per repair. I was happy and the homeowner was happy. Win, Win situation with repairs. If I came across a repair that I didn't have a part for, I would make sure I picked some spares for another job. So besides my basic gutter cleaning equipment, I also carried an inventory of repair parts I might need. Along with some basic tools to do repairs.

Some basic repair tools I carried : Cordless drill, 1/8 inch drill bits, rivet gun and rivets, hammer and assorted aluminum or galvanized nails, wire cutters, standard and Phillips screw drivers, hack saw, gutter seal.

Chapter 7

Chapter 7

How to Clean Gutters

Now I know this isn't rocket science, but I'll remind you of that old saying," any job worth doing is worth doing well". If you hold yourself to higher standard people will take notice, and it's a direct reflection on you and your company.

What I consider the proper way to clean gutters is as follows .Lets say I showed up on a job for a two story colonial with an attached two car garage. I always set my ladder up on the highest gutter, on the corner of the house opposite the addition right where the downspout is. Clean out corner of gutter and flush downspout with hose. Make sure the elbows are clean of any debris. Clean out everything in gutter that you can safely reach. Use hose to spray down cleaned area. Now use your gutter debris rake to push as much debris toward the middle of the gutter. Doing this will save you a lot of time repositioning ladder. Keep hosing down cleaned areas as you go along. Once you reach the middle of the gutter, start at the opposite corner and repeat. On this corner the higher gutter may drain into the lower one, the lower gutter on the garage may need to be cleaned first, depending on how jammed up it is. You won't be able to flush the higher gutter if the lower is jammed up. Everything that you remove from the gutter should be put in some sort of pail and taken away from jobsite. As your cleaning, you should also be inspecting for repairs that need to be done. Repeat same process on opposite side of house.

The re-positioning of the ladders, and climbing up and down the ladders is what takes the most time on a cleaning job. I always tried to work as efficiently as possible, while still being safe.

Have you ever noticed the amount of products that have been invented to assist the homeowner in cleaning the gutters, or to try to completely eliminate gutter cleaning? It is definitely an indication that cleaning the gutters is one the most dreaded, foul, dangerous home maintenance jobs that most homeowners try to avoid. I would always come across some sort of device that was utterly useless. Plastic screens stand out as one of the worst culprits. Whenever I came across these I would tell the homeowner that there would be no charge if I could just tear them out and throw them away, but if I had to take them out and re-install them, it would cost more, much more. I have also come across gutter covers, it's usually some type of metal cover that's permanently installed and there's only a small opening to get at debris, usually only an inch or two. Now try and get into the gutter to clean it out, complete nightmare.

The fact of the matter is that most devices either don't work completely or just don't work as advertised. Which means eventually the homeowner will come to their senses and call in a Professional Gutter Cleaner.

Chapter 8

Chapter 8

Final Thoughts

As you may have noticed, I haven't showed you any business models or theory of business, or algebraic formulas. My only rule was to have more money coming in than was going out. Making $50,000 yearly part-time was really simple. I live in the Northeast U.S. so the gutter cleaning season is usually 8 to 9 months long. Usually March to November. Let's assume there are 34 weeks in the season. To make $50,000 yearly I only had to make about $1500 per week for 34 weeks, or another way to calculate it is:

Monday   6 jobs

2 capes @ $75 ea.

2 colonials @$150 ea.

1 colonial @$150 plus 2 repairs @ $25 ea.1 split entry @$100

Monday total $750

Tuesday 4 jobs

1 cape @$50

1 colonial @$125

1 colonial @150

1 multi-family rental property @$200

Tuesday total……………………………...............................$575

<u>Wednesday and Thursday 1 job</u>

Townhouse complex @ $1500

Wednesday and Thursday total……………………………….$1500

Total for week……………………………….............................$2825

Friday Saturday Sunday- Gone Fishing, took cell phone and daily planner along to schedule next weeks work.

  Some weeks I worked 7 days, others I worked 2 or 3 days. I hardly ever worked 7 days a week, it was usually a 4 day work week, and I had the winters off. Being able to make your own schedule is one of the best parts of being self-employed.

  Well, I hope you enjoyed my book, I know it is a quick read, but hopefully it has sparked your entrepreneurial spirit. Good luck,

W.H.Griffin

www.ingramcontent.com/pod-product-compliance
Lightning Source LLC
Chambersburg PA
CBHW021039180526
45163CB00005B/2202